CASEY AT THE BAT

With one more inning left, the score is four to two and Mudville is losing. Somehow they manage to hold on so that the mighty Casey can have his turn at bat. He approaches the plate, acknowledges the crowd's cheers, casts a defiant eye in the pitcher's direction and takes his stance. Casey is ready. Surely he will save the day?

Ernest Lawrence Thayer's rousing verse and Wallace Tripp's clever characterizations combine in a splendidly colorful version of the classic baseball poem.

CASEY AT THE BAT

A Ballad of the Republic, Sung in the Year 1888

by Ernest Lawrence Thayer

illustrated by Wallace Tripp

Coward, McCann & Geoghegan, Inc.   New York

Martin Gardner's excellent and entertaining *The Annotated Casey at the Bat* is the source for this version of *Casey,* which is exactly as it first appeared one Sunday morning in June 1888, in the San Francisco *Examiner.*

Illustrations copyright © 1978 by Wallace Tripp

LIBRARY OF CONGRESS CATALOGING IN PUBLICATION DATA

Thayer, Ernest Lawrence, 1863-1940.
   Casey at the bat.
   SUMMARY: A narrative poem about the celebrated baseball player who struck out at the crucial moment of a game.
   1. Baseball—Juvenile poetry. [1. Baseball—Poetry]
I. Tripp, Wallace. II. Title.
PZ8.3.T25Car   811'.5'2   LCC 77-21199
ISBN 0-698-20486-7 (paperback edition)
First Peppercorn paperback edition published in 1980.
Typography by Cathy Altholz
Printed in the United States of America

The title was set in Quentin and other display type in Primitive. The text type was set in Century Old Style and the book was printed by offset at Rae Lithographers.

The outlook wasn't brilliant for the Mudville nine that day;
The score stood four to two with but one inning more to play.
And then when Cooney died at first, and Barrows did the same,
A sickly silence fell upon the patrons of the game.

A straggling few got up to go in deep despair. The rest
Clung to that hope which springs eternal in the human breast;
They thought if only Casey could but get a whack at that—
We'd put up even money now with Casey at the bat.

But Flynn preceded Casey, as did also Jimmy Blake,
And the former was a lulu and the latter was a cake;
So upon that stricken multitude grim melancholy sat,
For there seemed but little chance of Casey's getting to the bat.

But Flynn let drive a single, to the wonderment of all,
And Blake, the much despis-ed, tore the cover off the ball;

And when the dust had lifted, and the men saw what had occurred,
There was Johnnie safe at second and Flynn a-hugging third.

Then from 5,000 throats and more there rose a lusty yell;
It rumbled through the valley, it rattled in the dell;
It knocked upon the mountain and recoiled upon the flat,
For Casey, mighty Casey, was advancing to the bat.

There was ease in Casey's manner as he stepped into his place;
There was pride in Casey's bearing and a smile on Casey's face.
And when, responding to the cheers, he lightly doffed his hat,
No stranger in the crowd could doubt 'twas Casey at the bat.

Ten thousand eyes were on him as he rubbed his hands with dirt;
Five thousand tongues applauded when he wiped them on his shirt.

Then while the writhing pitcher ground the ball into his hip,
Defiance gleamed in Casey's eye, a sneer curled Casey's lip.

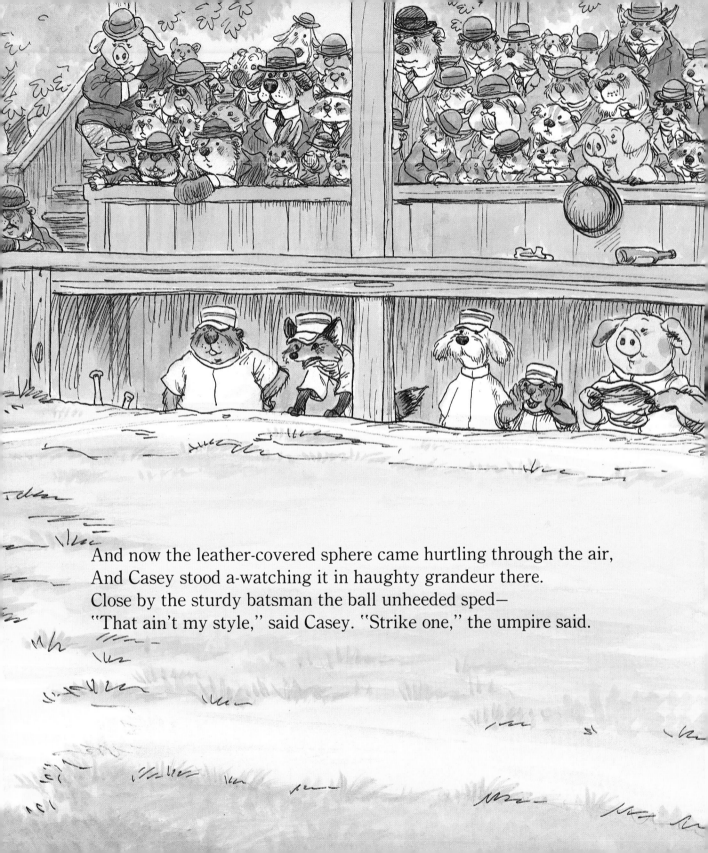

And now the leather-covered sphere came hurtling through the air,
And Casey stood a-watching it in haughty grandeur there.
Close by the sturdy batsman the ball unheeded sped—
"That ain't my style," said Casey. "Strike one," the umpire said.

From the benches, black with people, there went up a muffled roar,
Like the beating of the storm-waves on a stern and distant shore.
"Kill him! Kill the umpire!" shouted some one on the stand;
And it's likely they'd have killed him had not Casey raised his hand.

With a smile of Christian charity great Casey's visage shone;
He stilled the rising tumult; he bade the game go on;
He signaled to the pitcher, and once more the spheroid flew;
But Casey still ignored it, and the umpire said, "Strike two."

"Fraud!" cried the maddened thousands, and echo answered fraud;
But one scornful look from Casey and the audience was awed.
They saw his face grow stern and cold, they saw his muscles strain,
And they knew that Casey wouldn't let that ball go by again.

The sneer is gone from Casey's lip, his teeth are clenched in hate;
He pounds with cruel violence his bat upon the plate.

And now the pitcher holds the ball, and now he lets it go,

And now the air is shattered by the force of Casey's blow.

Oh, somewhere in this favored land the sun is shining bright;
The band is playing somewhere, and somewhere hearts are light,
And somewhere men are laughing, and somewhere children shout;
But there is no joy in Mudville—mighty Casey has struck out.

It was my fellow illustrator, Jan Adkins, a regular fountain of verse, who suggested between recitations that a new version of Casey was long overdue and that I ought to give it a try. And so I did, and here it is.

For me, Ernest Lawrence Thayer's vintage piece of Americana, even after countless readings, never ceases to be funny and never loses its last-line clout—or is it swat? The poem is a clever joke, reversing our expectations and bursting a balloon in the best comic tradition, but perhaps what makes it endure is the way it is built on the character of Casey and the crowd. Exaggerated and whimsical the poem may be, but it is also universal and "true." Ernest Lawrence Thayer was a philosophy major at Harvard, and later a journalist. The fame of *Casey at the Bat* during Thayer's lifetime was not entirely pleasing to him. He would no doubt have preferred to be remembered for something a bit more exalted, but as the poem has assured him some small piece of immortality, I can't feel very sorry for him!

—Wallace Tripp